# Imagination Drawing Station

WELCOME! My name is **Captain Creativity**. I am happy
to Invite you to my **Imagination Drawing Station**. This booklet contains
a series of drawings that are incomplete. Your task is to finish these drawings using
your imagination in the most creative way possible. I call it "imaginating". There are three types
of incomplete drawings in this booklet.  They are:

1.  **Shapes Task** – This page will be filled with a series of the same shape (all circles, or all squares, etc.).  You will need to sketch objects or pictures which have that shape as a major part of the completed picture. For example, if the page is filled with circles, you must imagine and draw as many objects as you can think of that would include a circle as the main part of the picture (glasses, smiley face, sun, wheel, etc.).

2.  **Incomplete Figure Task** – This page will have only one shape, form, or line on it. You will need to use that figure as part of the most unique, elaborate, imaginative drawing you can think of. You should try to include elements such as emotion, humor, movement, have it tell a story, etc. Try to be as original as you can. You will also need to come up with a title for your picture, that too, should be original and imaginative.

3.   **Story Task** – This page will contain the start of a picture. You will be asked to imagine and draw what you think is behind or inside the object that is drawn. Your drawing should tell a story without words that is original and creative, full of imagery.

**NOTE TO PARENTS:** After the next page, I will show you  how you can
help your child use this booklet to explore and expand their creative abilities.

**A Creative Mindfexors® Workbook**

# Examples:

Shapes Task

Incomplete Figure Task

Story Task

# PARENTS: *How to Nurture Creativity*

The Imagination Drawing Station is based on one of the most iconic elements of the Torrance Tests of Creative Thinking — the Incomplete Figure Task. For a child to be able to utilize the fullest extent of his/her creative ability, it helps for him/her to know what constitutes creativity, so they can more fully explore it. Creativity is not how well the picture is drawn, more importantly it is what is represented by the drawing. I have listed out the criteria researchers use to measure one's creativity in these tasks. Read through the list and as your child works through this booklet, give them examples of how they could give more detail to their drawings, in order to show emotion or movement or humor. Expand your child's creative-thought to include thinking of the drawing perhaps from a different perspective, or more abstractly. Help them dig deeper into their imagination to go beyond the most logical way to complete the figure (for example: something other than a shark, when they see an open triangle), or a more expressive title for their picture. Above all, remember, to nurture is to be supportive. Compliment all of your child's efforts and use this list to suggest and cultivate, not demand. Enjoy watching your child's creativity grow!

- **Emotional Expressiveness:** Communicating feelings and emotions through titles and drawings. Facial expressions, gestures with hands, a tear, kissing, outstretched arms, etc.
- **Storytelling Articulateness:** Putting things in context; telling a story through the drawing
- **Movement or Action:** Showing action (rest, stand, sit, lie, run, etc.) either implying or stating action through the title or through the figure drawing (position of body, motion of lines)
- **Expressiveness of Titles:** Transforming visual information into emotions and feelings expressed in words (beyond simple description of drawing)
- **Synthesis of Incomplete Figures or Lines:** Combining two or more incomplete figures into a drawing
- **Unusual Visual Perspective:** Presenting ideas or objects in another view other than the one we would ordinarily see (above, below, at different distances, in an unusual position, etc.)
- **Internal Visualization:** Visualizing beyond the object (drawing it from the inside, or a cross-section)
- **Humor:** Incorporating unusual situations and surprises (exaggeration, opposites, satire, puns, etc.)

# Section 1: Shapes Task

This section will have pages filled with a series of the same shape (all circles, or all squares, etc.). You will need to sketch objects or pictures which have that shape as a major part of the completed picture. For example, if the page is filled with circles, you must imagine and draw as many objects as you can think of, that would include a circle as the main part of the picture (glasses, smiley face, sun, wheel, etc.).

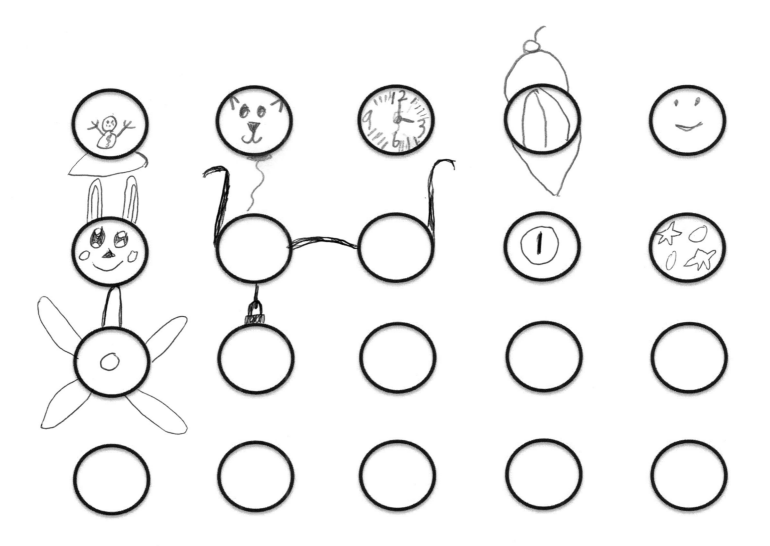

Shapes Task

Seasons greetings

Bb
Cc Aa

Shapes Task

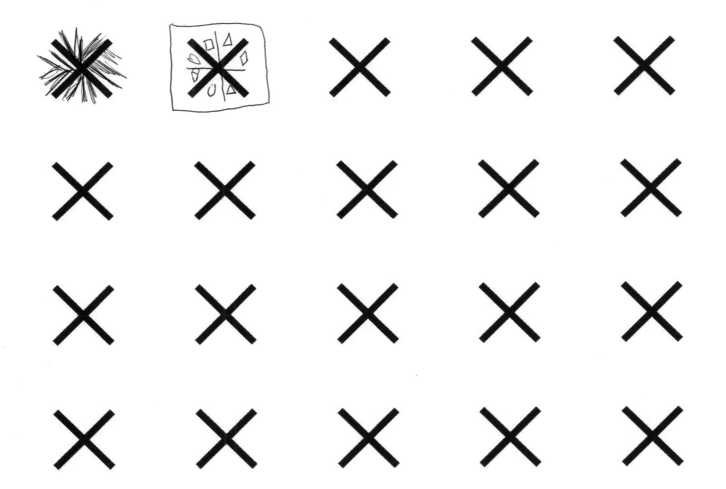

Shapes Task

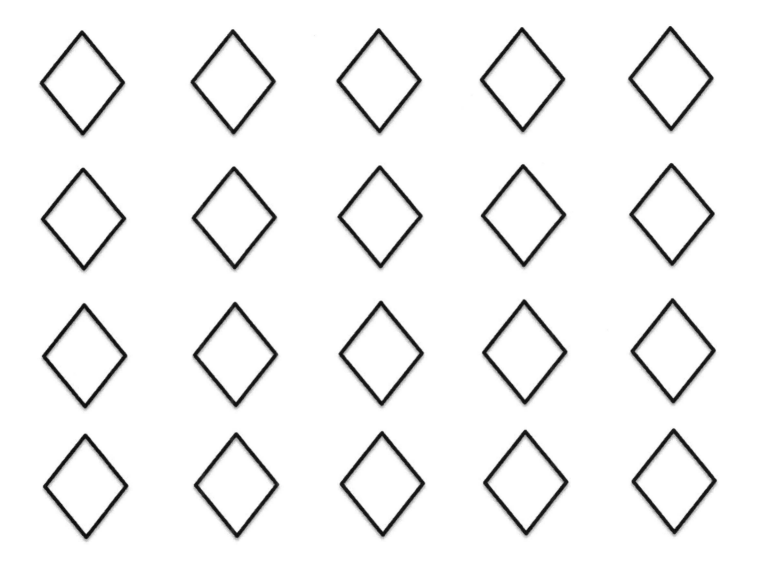

Shapes Task

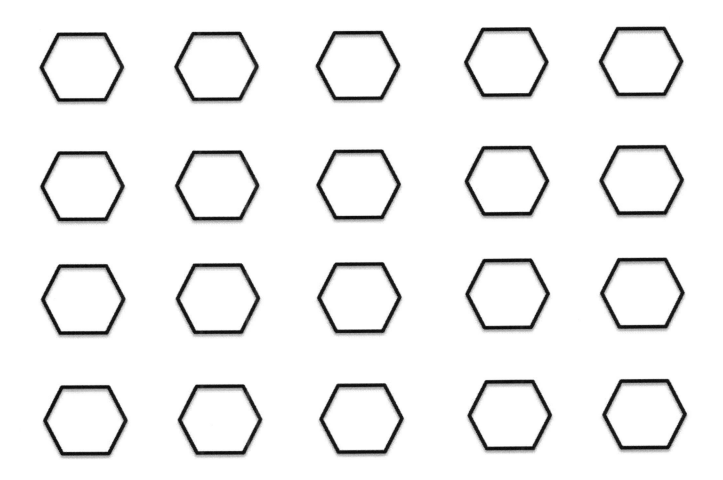

Shapes Task

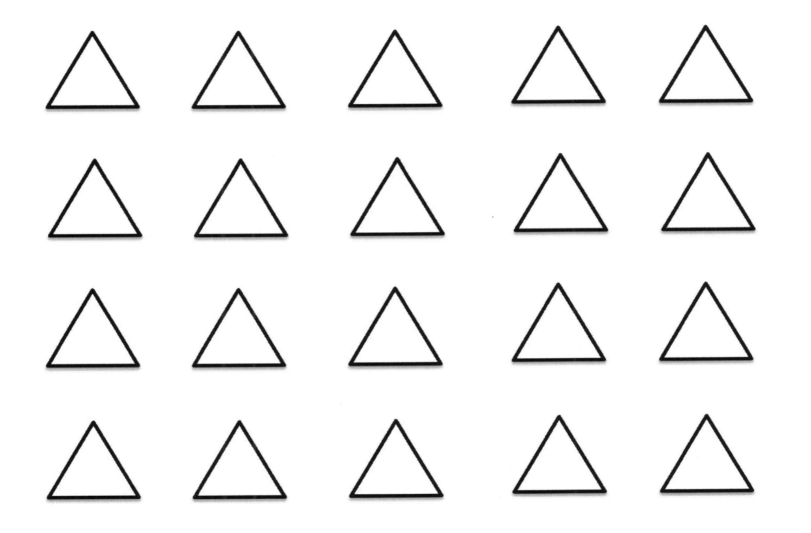

Shapes Task

Shapes Task

# Section 2: Incomplete Figure Task

This section will have pages with only one shape, form, or line on it. You will need to use that figure as part of the most unique, elaborate, imaginative drawing you can think of. You should try to include elements such as emotion, humor, movement, have it tell a story, etc. Try to be as original as you can. You will also need to come up with a title for your picture that too, should be original and imaginative.

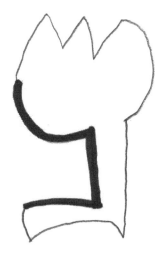

**Title:** flower char

**Title:** Ranbo chek

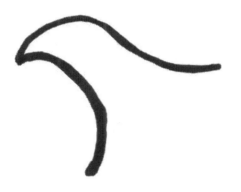

Title:_____

**Title:**_____

Title:_____

Incomplete Figure Task

Title:_____

Title:_____

Title:_____

Title:_____

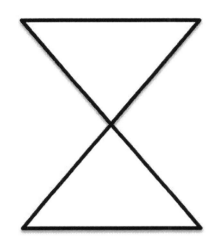

**Title:**_____

Incomplete Figure Task

Title:_____

Incomplete Figure Task

Title:_____

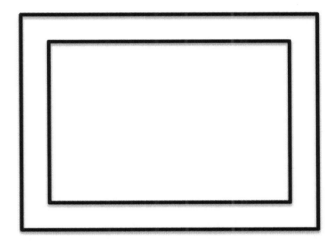

Title:_____

Title:_____

# Section 3: Story Task

This section will have pages that contain the start of a picture. You will be asked to imagine and draw what you think is behind, on, or inside the object that is drawn. Your drawing should tell a story, without words, that is original, creative, and full of imagery.

What's on the other side of this door?

Story Task

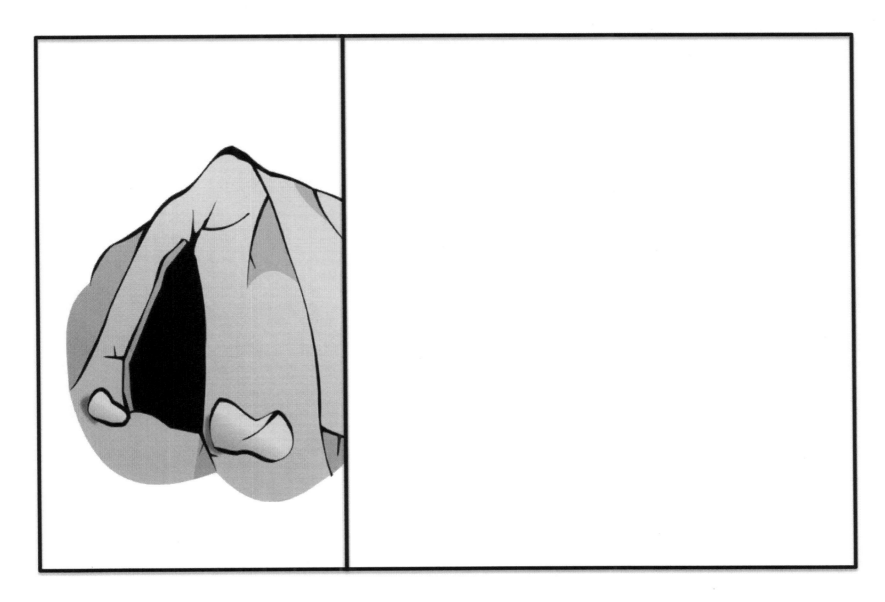

What's inside this cave?

Story Task

What's inside this spaceship?

Story Task

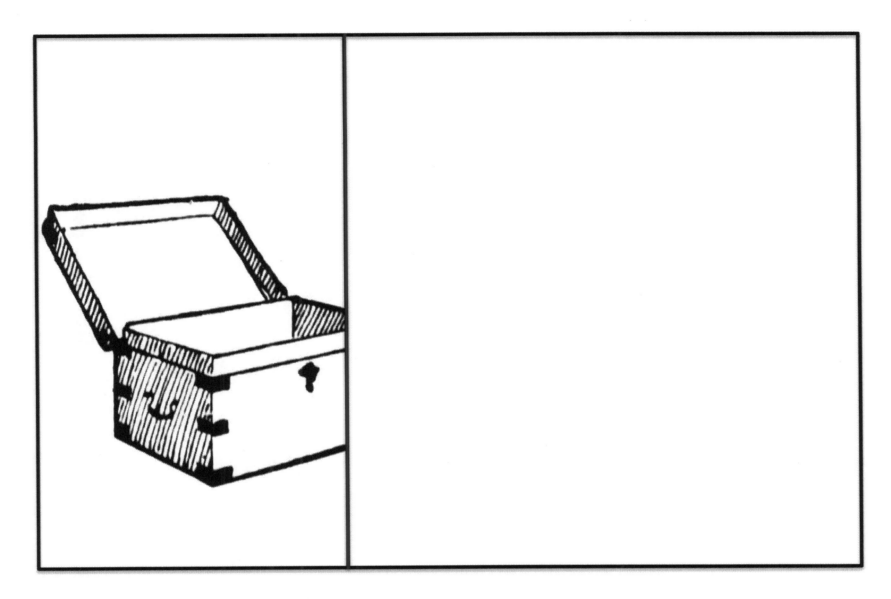

**What's inside this chest?**

Story Task

What's behind this wall?

Story Task

What's inside this tent?

Story Task

What do you see inside this window?

Story Task

What's inside this store?

Story Task

What image do you see in this mirror?

Story Task

What's inside this present?

Story Task

**Who lives inside this house?**

Story Task

What escaped from this cage?

Story Task

https://RaiseCreativeKidz.com

https://www.facebook.com/RaiseCreativeKidz

**Other Products Available on Amazon:**
- ➤ Creative Mindflexors® Cards
- ➤ Creative Mindflexors® Cards 2
- ➤ *Raise Creative Thinkers:*
  *A Guide to Developing Children's Creative Intelligence*